lovinggertrudestein loving Gertrude

LOVING GERTRUDE STEIN

by
Deborah Schnitzer

TURNSTONE PRESS

Turnstone Press
Artspace Building
607-100 Arthur Street
Winnipeg, MB
R3B 1H3 Canada
www.TurnstonePress.com

Turnstone Press gratefully acknowledges the assistance of The Canada Council for the Arts, the Manitoba Arts Council, the Government of Canada through the Book Publishing Industry Development Program and the Government of Manitoba through the Department of Culture, Heritage and Tourism, Arts Branch, for our publishing activities.

The Canada Council for the Arts | Le Conseil des Arts du Canada

Manitoba Arts Council | Conseil des arts du Manitoba

Canadä

Cover design: Doowah Design
Interior design: Sharon Caseburg
Printed and bound in Canada by Kromar for Turnstone Press.

National Library of Canada Cataloguing in Publication Data

Schnitzer, Deborah, 1950-
Loving Gertrude Stein / Deborah Schnitzer.

Poem.
ISBN 0-88801-297-7

1. Stein, Gertrude, 1874-1946—Poetry. I. Title.

PS8637.C45L39 2004 C811'.6 C2004-900949-4

to the students Woolf'nStein,
merry makers of the beautiful at the University of Winnipeg

Happy thanks to Sharon Caseburg—careful, sure, expert—and Todd Besant, and Kelly Stifora at Turnstone who make this long layering possible. To Mandy Malazdrewich for the photograph of the me I see, Terry Gallagher for the just-perfect pigeons, Heidi Harms for her thorough reading of page proofs, Donnelly Smallwood for our work in "paper weight" and Bob Haverluck for the "rifting" of blue.

To my own sweet, slightly mad family—Mendel, Ben and Zach, my friend Michael . . . Always, we carry each other along.

lovinggertrudestein loving Gertrude

(set in slides on time

gradual l y
I am ma de

so

in space)

\ landing in paris in any given spring my spring
runs
into 27 rue de Fleurus

my old lover trailing doggeddy I know because and the
way evenbefore the pavement I amtelling
here it must be where I am

my mother Inez has not g on e

toparis though she dreamed   green
wanting herown wingsp r e a d

I did not bring her

this here of heaven partially understood an opening
I could
and my mother who never flew
(though gifted
stayedstupid in the almost crazy
of a white woman over
looking
her potential
thinking the river welcome always unjumped never across

I left   living longer than   she thought   I
should
left

with such as one she'd bitten in her sleep
bad as

any apple

married

this one

lifting bellybig
book bold and
lettering

g

g
r
a
d u al t ill I am

and would I sound her this way if
in the rue de Fleurus   Inez   came to (o)
her round
in   my neck

(this sight I make   insist upon)

[gertrudestein to Inez Miriam Pearl all most lovingly]
the goodies of hello hello   look Alice   who is he/reher e

[Inez fumingly]
damned nonsense you
c ouldn't be
me **[gertrude quick]**
and you the french for nose I saynezz not neigh notnis   how
did that happen   nescient   in such a small   town

the Soo? **[trialed Inez res/trains gertrude's field day]**
you think you   come differently

[cue d]
from pennsylvania always the allegheny I do tellspeling l w/elle
wel ll

[foaming]
for heaven's sake gertsayrude your own thick sound set in that t/hat ri
di cu lous vest babyovergrowncradlecapsalon

I've heard money given to you gobs of it

[grin to alice gapingless   morethan she ought runso gertrude driving does not reverse]
ba by   bB a b e   bé bé

[firing stillInez in pain points to Inez again]
don't   my daughter   loves you more   saysso in   her
life which she thinks   passed/t me

[fond free gertrude seizes]
yohooyou Inez say no there in your stout heart pianofingersbit ten-
down   not enough brave   living too long with only one alas   your
elephant unbeaten by candy
some nothing coming out of you

rift

(slack   (like the brother)

True   my mother's bicker   tailedher

(me trying to stand
myself in/differently)

airplanedspring flying from   vancouver son twenty one
I say my love in depart start   le speak steinese
mouthmaking   he catches   our crooked release
tearstained ripe we are   glory in the
come   and go

I carry   motherwonder sweetsay love I love
                    his shygoodbye

                   I could
                      better
                      wanting less than she asked (for this
                                                                 mother
                                                                 mine st ill
                                                                 t r a   v
                                                                                e
                                                                                l
                                                                        s
                                                                 s

parts

(First(story first

I am going to develop love   onpaper
weight you didn't
have

so
fearful   of the body   you   would bring

out of me

yourrare name
folds
into
fingers a
p/liant dusting
blinds   I print
mythighs bring you back
though   I   broke your water
still born
you splashagainst my breast
let me look at you
ru n   n i

n

g

I

c/ouldn't
imagine you except as
disappointment
impossible
L
o
o
k
i
n
g
Glass wars of dependency
the storm of you
beachcollected in pieces
waterworn
carrying glass
I
d
i
d
not discover the sound of you no
grateful for af ter
now
I
look for

you end u/re

where

you
travel
in me
west
there
with your father
m
o
n
e
y
some
graduate school   *fear*
I passed we turned   *into*
north
for a long time
we
didn't have you   *thought*
better wait   *\s   ee*
how
people had children
what they did with them
so they would not hurt

b
u
t
we
didn't
been ten

you would have

t
h
e
n

maybe
if
we had not but
moved a bit
after
to more school and long/e r long e r

papers
long enough

when the boys came
I thought
luck
how would I be if
thought only of what my little was
chubby wrong
I was you see and it made m
e very

temper
theysay
bad didn't smile for

would

you

heav/ey

me too

<table><tr><td>extra
s who
determine /s
night night day</td><td>day</td></tr></table>

I think I saw a smile you might
I think I would
have under
stood

I think I saw a smile you might
I think I would
have under
stood
the sil/liness of beaches and pebblehunting
hunched as the pail handle toedigging to find the
pretties
I think we would have done that collecting
you in pieces printing you in
glass houses
stone throws
waterworn
into sing the
sound you
surface
you would have

                    be en
                      political
why
                      the billboards
                      we would have worked
                      them through to the
other side   found things   out
     you were probably
                  very
                clear about that wanting to know why and why and why a
nest   me too

(always I have that burning inside   my mouth)

I would have kissed you by the fire hel
d your hand I
your hand I

your fFingers
the way yourlittle one
c/rooks with a softer
inden/ta\tion by the second knuckle
I would have soaped lovingly
because
you must have dimples(that's
conceptual)
I would have embraced
every il/lusion you

toes
I would have been glad of your toes tender button
big toe bang for whenyou ran right into the iron boat hold on the
deck

boat h/old
I would have said Watch out for that sweetheart
(watch out for that sweetheart)
don't run s o fast and
off
but I would have known how to fix (would have
been

soft again and
ice cream
we would have double dips and you would talk
me into just one and j/ust once more and Chocolate
sprinkles and
that book
about because you knew how it worked
and I would

listen you could tell me things
I would ask you how

felt

if you were happy
I would have loved you
this much and mucher
er
I would not have seen you only as the unlovely parts of me twitching in the
drying sa/liva
on the beach
I you could have counted
on me

two parts
    (in/ one
        counting paris paris

\from son to son in
voices Fflying so my own

me nest/led in

along love looking
intwo languages/me
sane loft liquid lettingdown hello breasting some say
Where Inez pulled her hair out
I
stay

in

p ag es

up

the seeing of a far ticket taken up   buckle
and away of imagining gertrudestein in paris inside my
head spreading spokens to
        speak   in g

t   s
f   i
i   n
wide l   la n g   u
a ge

F
f   l ng me in the everywheretimezones of those who
i
seeing sing   \ s/arnes
and so
and so
thus and thus

I

o s

d e

e

y

flyeying me (f)l

my f (lie) in the every where of space

s/pace

and steinagain

the sheer Pic

as so

o f It

the doing and done

beauty ofit

so they would say and believe yes they wou ld
could
stand
stir red
(where(is that/this rhyme in time from somewhere) else
singing ether in me/loving Gertrude Stein in me/when
I
a
mstuck

the backwhens

t(h)ings
that
sta y

nside
buttonbitsbed
dingburst sunstraw
shelled beautiful

<u>art</u>

\ lovinggertrudesteins inone
each alice

every time a k/new time
meeting analice anew
so m/anylikeness/nes
sting likingshedsl
iedowns
gertrudesittings
lookinglikePicassopaintinggertrude
Ll/i/king
looking
lesslike
more than
e g g s
two bodies
loving
loving
one care/ fully
sleeping
so the other wakes
andmakes
in the beautifulbeautiful
words looking for love fwound in mornings of
this gertrudegertrude
s\ay alices

t)here

there
(there
w/would be
thegood
and good bye
sweeteas of
hello
Ccheeky
backstroking
the
h
and waking wonderfuls

word   fan

count   me   in cro/ssing
l   eft and
left
behind   rounding
sound
Into
seep
to In
stru
m
e
n
t ripening love   perhaps stay in the early
early bird song sung to say   come
lookwindows
like
like
one side and   one   side
un/sided inside sound   sailings
calling virgin into wake   a
virginia wriinkling

partings

(me opening my interlude
showing silent
say seeing gertrude a rising
the lovely gertrudesteining
and
a
l
i
c
es

roo | t ing for

1. when
   (does the rhythm find me)every time/2.newtime/3.half-
    open eyetime
    van Gogh'n
    me   husky   b

a

5. the edge of line curling   ck ears opening inside moving   me
churchlike

2. (where does gertrudestein find me and where do I keep her
   for getting)
1.   another language writing in the long time line of it
back and talk
so they say
inthe so you say and believe 2. In the lying down lap of it 3. In the
press of those parts of it that make love
    sweeties

gertrudedips into **ink sp/re a d s**
as pages in my
barn
the liquid lost of it she bites
through succulent lounging at the door   lace
leaking

windowed
in this way
in this way
such a turn for it

such a stroking of the fur shaving and the body as
cream blade running cheap shot images

notatelier
but suite d so   sweetly self   conscious
the here of clever
                    these men coming
this
loving   gertrude stein
losing   her in the every day

that making   of the living
that shortness   of the view
turning a way from   again
and
a
g
a
I
n

lost in syllable
s

taking temperature
s

finding me my friends
Under the bed

3. dusting Arles
sluts wool on the tip of tongueyou are when I am loving

gertrudestein
fired (1,2,3) moving across
pageflying a side habit s of my belt pulled
in direc tly
I am thinlight

water does t hat
for women
over50
who exercise
in pools together

I am not condomed
in this
me skinning dipping
ink welled loving gertrude
stein half lost in the
tuning scales

of
an old world
o
p
en
in
g

parts three me

a
cross section
jesus   bent again
this me playing gertrude stein badly is still
      me
      playing gertrudesteinscaling s tilts
everything Pi   sa h
tourists
yes again the wind and into/ swept   hair for any   occasional
   Imagine
I don't like to fuss wanting the feeds perennial the once again andonce
more loving gertrude stein who gardens me
on behalf and behold
seated not defeatedand not
myself

a very good gardener can
talk   move require

in the stalking of pe
on
ies
any i
n
k/c
line warming
defer evenwhen a m taken by
t umbling d
o
w
n
a rest amo n gg

Ifeel the loss of a single stein(ein)

a rosing (have friends who say it)
better
but fond lush and trailing
dis
order dis
cover
this sea surface that profusion which hits
any 15th century sonnet
I do
my fallin g d
o
w
n
n my head for
untumbled I must be lest the
laying do
own
claim the lives
of the surface
effects in the
virginia l
anguage running in very
colour in every
departing t/his pink and still this p/ink here

one words tra/vel l iii ng

finding me in this anygarden the first and the second of it
                    loving gertrude stein losing touch
        coming back to the painted daisy petal counter
        loves me
        loves me

whose chances

why that order

/

1. I am

dispositioned

finding and finding again

who loves me

even when the loving of me is not my idea

when the hand weakens

and the body falling down as yours is

the loss

the loss

takes me

\

2. could I not be
still
exchanging liquids

that watering
so grow
the begin of alas

even if the when of you is gone
I will

remembering backward
the autobiography of neverwas and was   is true tok/las

3.curls
I think you have had some
maybe wave y/es
probably that
      and sweet
oh your eyes they would have found me rooms would have made m
ore sense because you would have and I

oh
I   miss you
    trave/l lessoften   do not travel well

    cut
    breathed out   when maybe
                                                just

(coming back to me mymoreparis seeing you)

surely
this is also loving
In the GertrudeStein at 72   40years
with Ali/ces
so many
places at once
serving gertrude'sending
how to be
in that
younger
with a nose of less

nothing remark/able   carrying
crosses of my mothers aging
times taken out on
me reading
tenses   losin   g

alice
turning to the dying
gertrude
soon   to be gone
but never
bowing once to the brother grudged at street
level
sir
lying better in
heronlyalice herevery be cause
treas u ring alice typed Gertrude
repeatedly a full baby
prodigious precious
heart in

misses

(another)

rifts blue
coming round years later
this
thinking
thaw

remembering my
mind in the kitchen of that pointe aux pins this Inez
thinking

she is mad
so I say so
when the lids blind my blue
she drawsin
daring
me to
say just before she goes out

you hurt me
always
using me
always you smoking my tobacco
now

your
chain
smoking the fill that
bursts through the lattice d
en am el ed
red
sitting   you   pie
                                 eyed

bad day   bad mother

                         gooddaughter
                              chess

I won't play. HA!
                          your   madsummer
with spoonsful of your brain   missing
not me

not even

my best friend Susan in the
back kitchen

even she
cannot open your stubborn cupboard
and she could before
            you
                h o a r dst
                                        ick our smug backsto your gone

                spooning heat into the already too hots.ımmer

                we pie the afternoon you cloud in
                                                                the front p/ orch

(having read of dyin g))

the bre aking of t\he
he   art
th/e smell
the h   old
turned camphor
now

l
e
s

s

the opening up of that no
more that alice does bedturning into g/own
the almosts
trying too
find alice
l0vingertrudesteins all
a l
ong good
byes that no
\

funeral years before a chapel
before a door begins
garden name for this
e
~~w~~
sw e lling

unable to sl
leep

pain's t/here

dreaming fire

(seeing myself in)

drinking tea through

a straw which was not
(and I told you so)
playing the piano with jam spre/ead so that you
could hold the notes
scotchtape everywhere and me re-wrappingthe
present for Mildred
moments be fore

you were off

you would do
that

murmur can hear you sticking
my heart sounds like Iam carrying you longer than ninemonths

my body born
baby
swathed skins I used to see

my

self in

(a part ing

Inez carries her entrance up stairs
into my house
dying dark
an angry I can
                not

n/ames every day her last
for years
this dead already counted between u\s
the stairs a sto(o)p (counting bet/ween us

pulling my shadow   blind happens
                             she willnot see me   again
                                                           I am notnear
her yet standing right standing beside   with her death bed   carefully
                                                                m a d e

she sees others
holds court in twilight
gives me my third person   "she loved odd colours"
                                     smiling as she would tell

                                        I do love colours

                                                  Idi d

in her retro/
spective
missing parts
my son at the door
"Mom"
"It's Ben" I say
loving this sound she sees her father of the same name
her face a jewel in his eye
I remember this Ben

namecalling
comeback(s
body
t
a

g

claiming p arts

(spacing))

4. I have my passion
~~F~~from another way of say

(2: from who said that) from
3: the way I run melodies together
lacking precision
which
I believe Gertrude lost only because she could find

a g ain
s

ing

nt

ou

so many mounting s

gertrude would not have seen
me standing

by e
I
was not
Ernest a
women al lied
with moustaches pencilled one
n
e
c
k
c
urving another

in that time
people were
in stages

looking differently
in the same way

still
alasand loving gertrudestein
a las and baby looking up pouring over
her ilk

a
2.

where the jew in this/gertrude
I cannot find it
in the beyond of biography

the some ones
jewinme
looking for the jewingertrude stein
[in/a/side]jews do this

look for each other
the
jewographer

not finding gertrude necess
arily jewish
except perhaps
In the centrality gertrude suggests for we m ust f
eel
her christ b
reaking d
own a
nail to let
the christnotchrist that aids digestion
wordwaivers
the inevitability of discipleship inali ces
(th)ough there is but one Alice
a live at a time
and
I
knowing
presume

make less
gertrudemastering sames
repeating
herself her self
feeding the many and theone that is the me in

Iam
seeing her

she promises land
be hind

every
curtain
c/all in g

not	*ton*
that	*taht*
she	*ehs*
would	*dluow*
have	*evah*
known	*nwonk*

when I came byparis there
was a less of
me
to/
catch her
would have been an almost
s
pending an
occasional flash
occasions mi
nor
I could not have been
hung by her

Tthough framed many times under the

nail

of *f:rst* l ovewhere
Iam no longer say
myselfas *bei* ng
myselfb*u*t do still

["say for yoursake"]
1972

al/so occasion al ly

a no more storystory

Susan and I we say Shiiiiiit

we've cooked through
bypass stifflip trans/plant
parent brokens

nothing to it
but
it is/pie/crust that defeats us sticking even with the
                                        vinegar and egg
                                        yolk and cold water
                                        wax paper
                                        the every trick
                                        picked during the picking summers from
  Janet next door   Mrs. Christie in town   Helen
  whatshername who lives   behind
  crumbledstorefront
                            stuck

                                                                                my mother issuddenly

my mother is ssuddenly
here   and the dough expert
                    pastry hands smoothing stretchin g
"you never could"   "give me that"

                              finger fluting   e/xactingl/y

Susan "How did you"

                    nothing

        "do that?"

Susan and I and   pie perfect

the porch plates the mold she takes inside her striped house
coat
inside out I lose this
madwoman cupboard full of
shoo
basket casket case
frozen pie
I almost die
thawing
the ten years
it
t(a)kes to
say
there was this courage in the pie\mad\making hand
thatholds serrated
kitchentable cooking

even when you could not see me floured beside
your/crust purple with unspokens
even then
I am saying when
we made pies together that summer we
did
not
die

(a not her)

misses in stein
conjure
for loving gertrudeStein
is

displaymea (n)t
and loving
gertrudestein
is
falling
d
o
w
n
in p/arts

re
ar ran
ging

making my self in this
    thinking of Gertrude' s lip/s
                                        tuck   oh
(oh)

a ny colour stays holding me in plastic
c oated c ases of the p lum m y mothers
d rew themselves up in
m aking me
    wait stretching
in the pollyesther of '61
o
  Gertrude did not wear this love song
sang pictures in
gypsy suits
feather
some boa

gertrude agarden
lost in
magnificent
play
playful
shethinking
asparagus and
t aking the 7 years so
they say of the harvest
to end this first movement

and there were others
before the first and
after the seventh
with out rest
instein
but I will
not tell
her
no
n e ver

what rue de landagain
land again

(A RECORDING OF IT)

they should have known each other and of course they
knew each other would be fools not to picnic
vinyl plates needle nest
service for two gramaphonally

one headcap
thicklipped drumbone
so da

another headcap
th/inner reed
st/raw

such types

hello virginia may I call you virginia and should I cap that if I do wouldn't you
why gertrude, you're gertrude. I saw you coming in my work. Lettuce?
Yes it feels like that I must say I do not read so many novels un less their writers bring them to me
Are you so much then in the centre of it?
my ear hears so all sorts find a friend in   more wine
But only for a time . . . Isn't it true that you
oh tootoo virginia here is the come and go of it which is what I wish

such chews

Always?
always
Doesn't it hurt when you are left then? No thank you
the unpublished I do not allow if the door is closed on that way out I am opening it
I do not butler my love as well.
oh yes you do but you call it differently
Do I do
that yes you call your work which is such come and go I have a recording of it
How nice. Asparagus?
oh yes and it's fine isn't it fine the way I do that

eating grassy

And you've read all of me?
oh no
Which ones?
the lines below your brow the ones you wished for bookselling
Thank you.
well it is the work is it not after all it is work and the work working
So often and then. White or read?
even moreso speaking louder than I can
That's what I've heard.
oh not only the rose is a rose is a rose
This clock you use is all tick and tock then?
yes every time why thank you
I was trying for the repeats (under changing).
which you do so

stained for good

You are brave in the way you show it and then don't let in any other.
you as well
But my essays more frequently admired
more familiar
But not
no no never by themselves always held by bottoms
That pond?
and not that pond
Never american only?
Oh never never american only why I come to paris every day
Yes. Sugar?
you
Oh I to vista, always to vista.

stained for good

and the setting of the table
You like her? Prunes?
your mrs. ramsay
She would do and could she
love the lily
such a round you give it.
the very virgin laid my way with words
we are friends then and I may call you gertrude
oh virginia these are the names for things are they not and why
wouldn't
you

all rubbings mouth made

one parts again

Inez   someme
in the kitchen   her arrangement kitchenas oysterhers
cooking fat   sticky love pulled apart in arguments
in front of a fat fridge

which she points to she points to   herself
narcissistic ally
wild cats on top of her fridge streaking our faces when in the lit
tle lit tle of am/we are opened always hungry

we cry if with held
    die
eating
her cut
    let
    b utter fed
    b rood born

hertalk of fine things springs she could
though I cannot talk to her again nor make her sound come round
in the cup sh e stir red in me her
sayings/sometimes come with bitter less
dream
she said
give
she said
think she said when she could
dress herself
when there were pills and chocolate bars round
her bed all her strawberry jams
crackers she was red

but bold in and some times out
could grab her piano swallow it
to make the something coming
follow
clear soup her strain hope
ful
(s)she rubs my cup reading
I am more
such chance to s e e debbiedoolie nestlingname

when the chocolate
came down all sorts
basted bylonesome /less
she might dear me

fourth part she

3. Ah/

there is this woolf

there is

this wrinkle and interlude figure

rising grey into sapphire and sun

I am the one waving

and she one drowned

(a Stevie Smith but

I saw it)

am so

am

shriven forgiven

whereas Woolf would

not [and cannot]

[call her Virginia]

one voice rum

inating

t

h

i

n

low c
louds
puffed
longjacketlongerarms longerfingerslongerlegslongerlonginglyall
along
she is
virginia
thinking
notseated
in a picasso
c
h
air

no
leaning/
desk ed she is

finding
the light harsh but necessary and the man who at
tends /dear /visioned with her in some of the very significant/

unable to excite too able to excite/watching her watch herself be
coming virginiawoolf nee stephens

and
to many of them doing good as females laced in reforma
toriestories with one-way windows streaming into the forest of
beyond their scope

submerge   din
subcutaneou sin
Under the   Sskin

of beadred heads talking writing walking round secluded and
occluded not she under   ling kicking   turf
skirted appalled outside the halls mur
mering
she simmering
she striking

out

voyages at all times of   day or
beginnings and departures mattering more and far out fins n
ot wasted for   water
(this too much echo in me)
where to find where to find the inside ear seashelled stories of
young men gone offslippered remembrances with pretty la
dies and the not   landing bottomed   o ut
teas and toasts in messy rooms/that'sengland after all isn;t it/form

faraway looks seedy and
somno lent

so saying think again
\
folds of highblood ladies hired show ceremonies
long ago ridiculous maintaining the

nothings of tradition simpering view s
coifed by highcollars
aimed
maiden heads Unstated and perversely
sewing listless encounters heavey brocades
trolley crossing fallingdowns

she made them cloud with murk and soured a/r/mour so
that percivals rowed themselves into oblivion on thames
and turkey and quiet men with all sorts of glassed
classicals sat silent rose petalled ri s
i
n g
g

short
term incandescent

oh

inside her stories I would be
night rocking in town towers of   I see
she marries me   to   inevitable

day light with
con scious

I could
say moment and room and beingI could say mary and marry, the
two asone stein made ofalice
Hidden in the sally forth   Sleep   Wake again as he she
gloss   dally

I swear she lives in every phrase   when I want   somethingsig-
nificant say
as time   fFly and space would lie
bottom \ boats by   trapped sun light
Stood trees
never touched but
Know by sight because
She
came and wrote them

pas/sing
pacing

the women that   Speckle eliot's come and go   she

where I am all scarves in the every which way of wind she sees
gathering for a centre
piece
just

holding
to make of
something seven sided,sixed she could stand so many ravellings

part

after

the work
upstairs in the
study   me   endless
underneath
should
washing machine
another meeting with
inside the car   (whose

car)
coverage because
in the afterall of   work in the world and the season
loving long/er
re   birth if it happens   depends mostly on the death
of stranger
how we're dropped off
once
these onces

she flied me this lovinggertrude
stalking her heart
in my hand
where the pen
egged the page night

she saw where I might feed

sow too
virginia pooling   teas me and the dying I saw ·where she
rocked a way   f/wound
lovelullabyes singing connect beneath goodbye
                                        sweetsadness liftingme
heart as breast to suckling book
                                        book to suckling heart
chest   rest ed
learning sound
s// waving
the victrola dug in the garden   any sp/ring(talk
                                                                        tel.ing rue
fleur

I   understand   (the spellings)   jonquil
and their rotation   forget me
spaced at   begonias n ea tly
nots
wider I am   s p r ea d

where there was so little   at first

a hired wet nurse
hosed
s/praybottle babies her
mothertired so stuck in her throat

twins at 40

four under three

pinched

who wouldn't
Inez all alonenoparis travelling
what I could not hold
held

mothernames you